Circus

Written by Daphne Ransom

Edited by Polly Hoffman

Illustrated by Sue Fullam

Cover Art by Denise Bauer

Teacher Created Materials, Inc.

6421 Industry Way

Westminister, CA 92683

www.teachercreated.com

©2002 Teacher Created Materials, Inc.

Made in U.S.A.

ISBN 0-7439-3063-0

Table of Contents

Introduction

Circus is a captivating, language-based, thematic unit. It has 80 exciting pages filled with a variety of cross-the-curriculum lesson ideas designed for young children. For each of the featured books, *Paddington at the Circus* and *See the Circus*, activities are included that set the stage for enjoyment of the book, and extending the specific concepts gained. In addition, the theme is connected to the curriculum with activities in language arts (including language experience and writing suggestions), math, science, social studies, art, music, and life skills (cooking, physical education,). Suggestions and patterns for bulletin boards are additional timesavers for the busy teacher.

This thematic unit includes the following:

❐ **Literature selections:** summaries of two children's books with related lessons (complete with reproducible pages) that cross the curriculum

❐ **Planning guides:** suggestions for sequencing lessons each day of the unit

❐ **Curriculum connections:** activities in language arts, math, science, social studies, art, music, life skills, and physical education

❐ **Group lessons:** activities to encourage cooperative learning

❐ **Circus links:** websites to connect to for additional information about the circus

❐ **Bibliography of related reading:** suggestions for additional books on the circus theme

❐ **Fine Arts:** suggestions for activities in music and art

❐ **Bulletin Boards:** suggestions for content-related bulletin boards

❐ **Home/School Connections:** suggestions for activities that could be sent home as well as performed at school

❐ **Culminating Activities:** suggestions for activities that require students to use what they have learned to create a final production to be performed for parents and other members of the school

---

Note: You may wish to punch holes in the pages and store them in a three-ring binder to keep this valuable resource intact so it may be used year after year.

Introduction *(cont.)*

Why a Balanced Approach?

The main advantage to using a balanced approach, is that it involves children using all modes of communication; reading, writing, listening, illustrating, and doing. Communication skills are interconnected and integrated into lessons that emphasize the use of language. Implicit in this approach, is our knowledge that every piece of language, including individual words, is composed of parts. Directed study of these parts can help a child master language communication. Experience and research tell us that regular attention to phonics, other word-attack skills, spelling, etc., develops reading mastery, thereby fulfilling the unity of the whole-language experience. The child is then led to read, write, spell, speak, and listen more confidently in response to a literature experience introduced by the teacher. In these ways, language skills grow rapidly, stimulated by direct practice, involvement, and interest in the topic.

Why Thematic Planning?

One very useful tool for implementing a balanced language program is thematic planning. By choosing a theme, with correlating literature selections for a unit of study, a teacher can plan activities throughout the day that lead to a cohesive, in-depth study of a topic. Children will be practicing and applying their skills in meaningful context. Consequently, the student will tend to learn and retain more.

Why Cooperative Learning?

Along with academic skills and content, children need to learn social skills. No longer can this area of development be taken for granted. Children must learn to work cooperatively in groups in order to function well in modern society. Group activities should be a regular part of school life and teachers would be wise to include social objectives, as well as academic objectives, in their planning.

Why Journals?

Each day your children should have the opportunity to write in a journal. They may respond to a book or an event in history, write about a personal experience, or answer a general "question of the day" posed by the teacher. The culminating journal provides an excellent means of documenting a child's writing process.

Why Big Books?

An excellent language activity is the production of big books as a whole class or in small groups. Groups of children, or the whole class, can apply their language skills, content knowledge, and creativity to produce a big book that becomes a part of the classroom library to be read and reread. These books make an excellent culminating project for sharing beyond the classroom with parents, librarians, other classes, etc.

Paddington Bear at the Circus

By Michael Bond

Summary

The beloved Paddington Bear has been entertaining children for many years. Once again, he amuses the reader when the circus comes to town! Paddington Bear can't wait to see the show under the big top. There's the ringmaster, a band, a very tall clown, and a man that hangs from a rope high above everyone's head. The ever helpful Paddington is always willing to lend a hand, and hurries off to save the distressed trapeze artist. The circus is turned topsy-turvy, but the show goes on, and Paddington Bear becomes the star.

Sample Plan

Lesson 1

- Introduce the unit by singing *Go To the Circus* (page 6, Enjoying the Book, #4).
- Read *Paddington Bear at the Circus* (page 6, Enjoying the Book, #1).
- Complete the maze activity (page 6, Enjoying the Book, #7).

Lesson 2

- Reread the story (page 6, Enjoying the Book, #6).
- Sing the song, "Swing So High" (page 18).
- Create a trapeze mobile (page 7, Enjoying the Book, #11).

Lesson 3

- Page through the story focusing on the clowns (page 6, Enjoying the Book, #3).
- Play the Bucket Balance Relay game (page 7, Enjoying the Book, #9).
- Create a tall clown (page 6, Enjoying the Book, #5).
- Teach the poem "Stilts" (page 31).

Lesson 4

- Review Lesson 3 on clowns, focusing on juggling.

- Create a juggling clown (page 6, Enjoying the Book, #2).
- "Let's juggle!" (page 7, Extending the Book, #4).

Lesson 5

- Perform the activity Draw Me a Story (page 34).
- Teach the poem "Clowns" (page 31).
- Complete the following directions activity (page 8, Extending the Book, #9).
- Review ending sounds (page 8, Enjoying the Book, #14).

Lesson 6

- Recite "Clowns" poem together (page 31).
- Review numbers and counting 1-3.
- Create a fun flap counting book (page 8, Extending the Book, #7).

Lesson 7

- Read another circus story (see Bibliography, page 80).
- Perform "Don't Burst the Balloon!" experiment (page 41).

Overview of Activities

Setting the Stage

1. Prepare one of the bulletin boards shown on page 71.

2. Make a child-size clown from sturdy cardboard or plywood, using the pattern on page 74. Attach one or two clothespins to the clowns chest or hand using hot glue or epoxy glue. Decorate the clown with paint, fabric, jewels, pom-poms, etc. Place the clown near the door or lesson area, and use the clothespins to "hold" the literature book that will be used that day, a practice sheet, or a special treat for all to eat.

3. Create one or more activity centers listed on page 72.

4. Play circus music in the background as the children work on projects through the unit (see bibliography on page 80).

Enjoying the Book

1. Show the cover of *Paddington Bear at the Circus*. Ask the children if they recognize the character pictured. Ask the students to predict what the story will be about. Read the story.

2. Teach the children the Juggling song on page 18. Make the Juggling Clown by reproducing pages 9 and 10 onto white construction paper. Each child will need one set. Ask the children to color and cut out both the clown and the juggling wheel. Lay the clown on top of the juggling wheel and fasten the two together by inserting a brad through the center dots. Sing the Juggling song while using the wheel.

3. Turn to the first page of the book. Ask the children with which circus performer Paddington was fascinated (the tall clown). Slowly, show the children the story, asking them to clap their hands each time they see a clown. Show each page with a clown and discuss how the clown is dressed and what he/she is doing.

4. Sing and teach *Go To The Circus* (page 62) while introducing the circus unit to your class. Draw the children's attention to a circus bulletin board (page 71) as you sing.

5. Here's a Big, or "Tall, " project the children will enjoy making. It will remind them of the circus character Paddington loved. Make decorations to represent the tall clown. Each child needs to make a silhouette, using his or her body outline. One at a time, ask each child to lie down on his or her back on a piece of butcher paper, three feet (91cm) longer than the child. Using a pencil or crayon, trace around the child's body, but don't trace around the bottom of the feet, the legs will be extended the extra length of the paper when the figure is cut out. After the child stands up, you may wish to retrace the pencil line using a thick, black, marker. Supply materials such as paint, markers, yarn, fabric, etc., and have each child decorate his or her body shape. Display tall clowns on the classroom or hallway walls. Teach the poem "Stilts" on page 31.

6. Reread the book focusing on the performing acrobats. Ask the children which acrobat Paddington thought needed help (the trapeze artist), and why. Ask if Paddington really did help and who helped Paddington get down.

7. Ask the children to help Paddington find his way to the circus by completing the maze activity, The Amaze-ing Circus, on page 13.

Overview of Activities *(cont.)*

8. Since leverage and balance help many circus workers perform, this is a great opportunity to introduce the concept of weight. Using scales, practice weighing objects from your classroom with your students. Be sure to point out that when an object is heavier, that side of the scale goes down. Show the students the page in the story where the acrobats are balancing on a ball. Discuss it. Collect the objects shown at the bottom of page 12 and weigh them on a scale. Hand out one copy of page 12 to each student and have them complete it as you weigh the objects in front of them. Children cut out and glue the object pieces in the correct place.

9. Let's play a balance relay game! Paddington thought the tall clown was going to dump water on him, but the bucket was empty. Children will enjoy trying to balance the bucket like the clown, before handing it off to a friend, in the Bucket Balance Relay game described on page 67.

10. Introduce the word "audience" to the students. Explain to the children that the audience is the group of people watching the show. Enhance your children's visual discrimination skills with the Animal Search worksheet on page 14. Give one copy to each child. Ask them to find and color the hiding animals.

11. Teach the song, "Swing So High," and then make the swinging trapeze mobile on pages 16-17. Each child needs one copy of pages 16-17, a 36" (91 cm) piece of yarn, an empty toilet paper tube, crayons, scissors, and a glue stick. Instruct the children to color the figure on each paper and cut it out. Put glue on the tab area of the bottom portion of the trapeze artist, then, lay the top portion of the figure on top to create the full body. Thread yarn through the paper tube and tie the ends together. Place the trapeze artist's legs around the paper tube and swing. Sing the song as the children swing the acrobat through the air.

Extending the Book

1. Teach or review opposites. Follow-up with the opposites match worksheet, Clowning Around With Opposites, page 33.

2. "Clowns" (page 31) is a funny poem your students will enjoy repeating over and over. Children make their own clown using pages 45-46. Copy one set of pages 45-46 per child and color and cut out the shapes on page 45. Build the clown by gluing the cut out parts onto the clown shape on page 46. It's a great way to review shapes too!

3. Review numbers 1-5. Ask your students to complete the counting activity on page 11. They count the scoops of ice cream, then draw a line to the matching numeral.

4. Allow the children to try juggling. Place beanbags, scarves, empty plastic pop bottles, or ping pong balls, in a special area in the classroom. Let the children practice juggling during free exploration time.

5. The show is about to begin! Introduce your students to telling time. Teach telling time to the hour and use the time match worksheet on page 44. Explain that when a circus comes to town, there may be as many as four performances each day. This way, more people can enjoy the show.

Overview of Activities *(cont.)*

6. Create two or three sets of high-walkers, or stilts, for your classroom by following the instructions on page 58. Allow the children to practice using them under adult supervision so they will be ready to perform on them in the culminating activity (page 68).

7. Children can make the fun flap counting book on page 15 to review numbers. Give each child one copy of page 15. Model for the class how to fold the paper in half, down the solid center line (numbers should still be showing). Next, model for the children how to cut along the dotted lines, top layer only. Instruct the children to lift flap #1 and draw one clown using their crayons. Continue lifting flaps and drawing the corresponding number of clowns. The students could draw circus animals if they would rather.

8. Turn to the first page of the story and ask the children what the clown is doing. Discuss what is on the poster and why the circus posters are used. Show real circus posters by logging onto a history site (page 80). Ask the children to design their own poster by using some of the ideas on page 59.

9. Put on a happy face! See how well your students can follow directions. Give each child a copy of page 35. Read the directions at the bottom of the page and ask the children to do what you say.

10. Play the Clowning Around relay game described on page 65. Give each student a copy of page 47 to complete after the relay activity. The children match the like tops and bottoms to the clown costumes.

11. Balloons are a colorful part of the circus and an inexpensive souvenir children may purchase and take home. That's why your students will enjoy watching the balloon inflate when you perform the simple experiment on page 41. Observe and discuss the results, then, have each student complete page 41.

12. This counting activity will surely make your students hungry. Brainstorm foods that could be purchased at the circus, for example; popcorn, peanuts, ice cream, cotton candy. Introduce simple addition using popped corn and shelled peanuts as manipulatives. Have the students complete the fun Yummy Facts worksheet on page 50. Use small cups of popcorn or peanuts as a reward for completing the activity.

13. Discuss a possible career, as a clown, with your children. Children do not think of clowning as being a real job, or a job that takes training and discipline. For more information on clown colleges, schools of circus arts, and physical theater, go to an Internet search engine and type in words such as: "clowns" or "clown college." Children can make the clown puzzle on page 57 after discussing the talented and ever funny clown.

14. Review ending sounds by doing the "Where do you hear the sound?" activity on page 32. Focus on the ending sounds of circus related words. End the lesson by having the children complete the Clowning With Ending Sounds activity on page 39.

Juggling Clown

Directions:

1. Color and cut out the clown on page 9 and the wheel on page 10.

2. Place the juggling clown on top of the wheel so that the two ★s line up. Connect the two together by placing a brad through the ★s.

Juggling Clown *(cont.)*

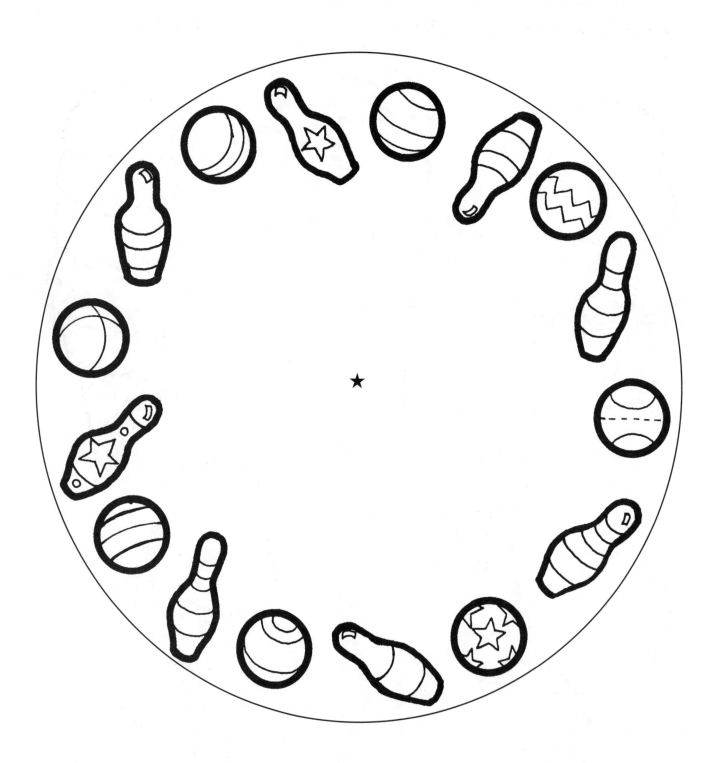

10

Ice Cream Count

Directions:

1. Count the number of scoops of ice cream on each cone.
2. Draw a line matching the ice cream cone to the correct numeral.
3. Color each scoop a different color.

Which Weighs More?

Teacher Preparation: Locate a scale and collect the objects shown below. Weigh the objects against each other in front of the class and discuss afterwards.

Directions: Color the pictures and then cut them apart along the dotted lines. Glue each picture in the column where it belongs.

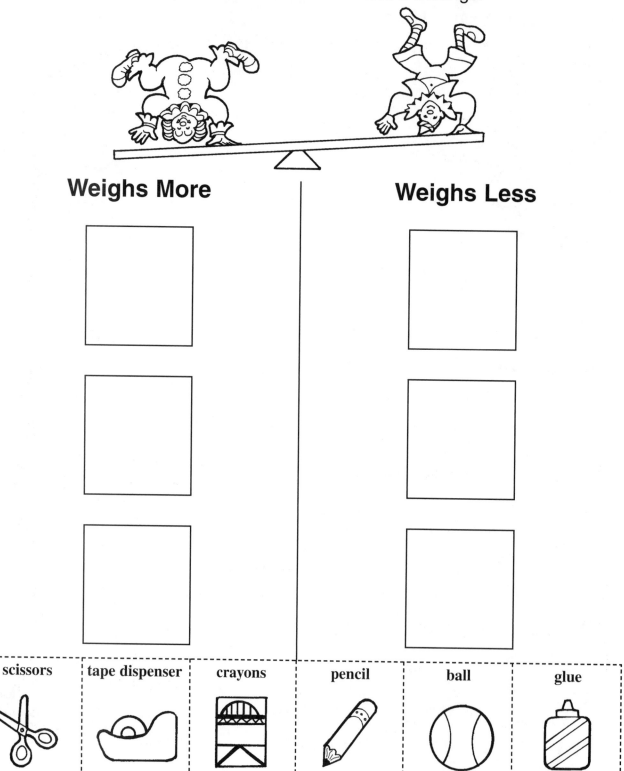

Weighs More

Weighs Less

| scissors | tape dispenser | crayons | pencil | ball | glue |

12

The Amaze-ing Circus

Directions: Help Paddington find his way to the circus tent.

Animal Search

Directions:

1. Look carefully at the audience.
2. Find and color the animals hiding among the people.

14

Fun Flap Book

Trapeze Mobile

Materials:

- one copy of pages 16-17 on white construction paper
- one 36" (91 cm) length of yarn
- one empty toilet paper roll
- crayons, scissors, and a glue stick

Directions:

1. Color and cut out the figures on pages 16-17.
2. Place glue on the tab of the torso piece and lay the bottom part of the body on top.
3. Thread the piece of yarn through the paper tube and tie the ends together.
4. Place the trapeze artist's legs around the tube and swing.

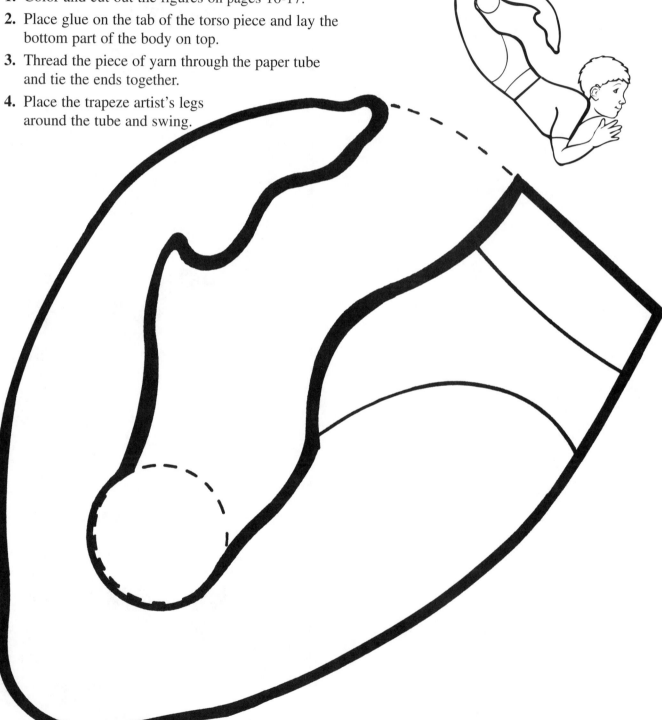

Trapeze Mobile *(cont.)*

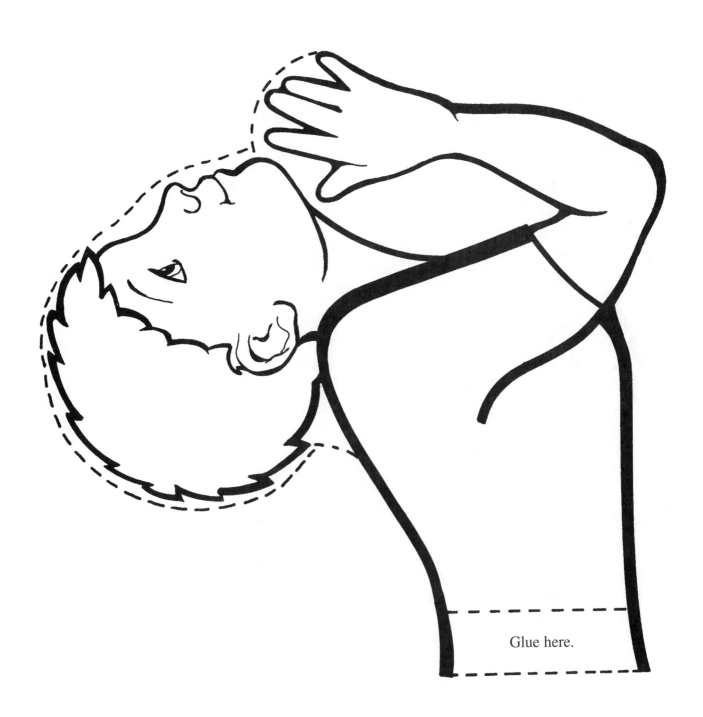

Glue here.

Paddington's Circus Songs

Paddington, The Circus Star

(Sung to the tune of "Clementine")

Paddington, Paddington
    You are such a silly bear.
You went up to help another
    And got caught up in the air.
Paddington, Paddington
    You are now safe on the ground.
The tall clown helped with his bucket
    And it made his pants fall down.
Paddington, Paddington
    You are now a circus star.
People laugh and cheer you on
    They come from near and far.

Swing So High

(Sung to the tune of "My Bonnie Lies Over the Ocean")

The trapeze flies over the circus
    It swings way up in the air.
The trapeze flies over the circus
    Oh, how I wish I was there!
Swing back, swing forth
    Oh, swing back and swing forth so high, so high!
Swing back, swing forth
    Oh, swing back and swing forth so high!

Juggling

(Sung to the tune of "I'm a Little Teapot")

Bowling pins and bean bags, scarves and balls
    Juggle them all but don't let them fall.
Start with one, then add some more
    Toss them up high, not drop on the floor.

     18

See the Circus

By H. A. Rey

Summary

This delightful story introduces children to the many wonderful performers of the circus. Children love this interactive lift-the-flap book because it is written in a guessing game format where the answers are revealed under the foldout flaps. Children will enjoy this book and its characters as much as they have loved H. A. Rey's beloved Curious George.

Sample Plan

Lesson 1
- Introduce and read *See the Circus* (page 20, Enjoying the Book, #2).
- Sing "Under the Big Top" (page 62).
- Create a classroom big book (page 20, Enjoying the Book, #1).

Lesson 2
- Choose a bell ringer activity (page 24).
- Reread the story (page 20, Enjoying the Book, #4).
- Teach spatial relationships (page 21, Enjoying the Book, #5).
- Make a riddle book (page 20, Enjoying the Book, #4).

Lesson 3
- Choose an estimation activity (page 24).
- Check story retention (page 21, Enjoying the Book, #7).
- Teach jump rope rhyme "Colored Balls" (page 67).
- Complete the color by number worksheet. (page 49).

Lesson 4
- Pretend to be a tightrope walker (page 22, Extending the Book, # 7).
- Teach the poem "Walking the Tightrope" (page 31).

- Create a movable tightrope walker. (page 61).

Lesson 5
- Choose a phonemic activity (page 32).
- Sing the alphabet song (page 22, Extending the Book, #5).
- Complete the dot-to-dot activity (page 37).

Lesson 6
- Choose a estimation activity (page 24).
- Discuss animals in the story focusing on the elephant (page 21, Extending the Book, #3).
- Perform the Elephant Walk (page 67).
- Create a Tent Raising picture (page 21, Extending the Book, #3).

Lesson 7
- Compare *Paddington Bear at the Circus* and *See the Circus* (page 20, Enjoying the Book, #3).
- Choose one or several physical activities (page 67).
- Sing "It's Here Again!" (page 62).
- Engage in a culminating activity (page 68–70).

Overview of Activities

Setting the Stage

1. Make a pointer to use when doing chart work or reading big books. Make a clown shape using the pattern on page 74. Color it and glue it to the end of an 18" long (46cm) ½" thick (1.5cm) dowel.

2. Prepare for a spatial relationship lesson (page 21, Enjoying the Book, #5) by running one copy per child of the Math Story Work Mat (pages 25-26) on construction paper. Cut out the pieces, mount onto tag board matching pieces together to create one scene, and laminate.

3. Make a Big Top Bottle described on page 58. Set out during free exploration time for the children to enjoy.

4. Run several copies of the circus patterns found on pages 73-75 on white construction paper. Place them in your art center along with a variety of art materials. Be sure to include craft sticks and encourage the children to make the figures into stick puppets.

Enjoying the Book

1. Create a classroom big book that your children can read by themselves. Enlarge the patterns on pages 30 and 76. Give each child a copy of page 30. Have each child write his or her first and last name in the blanks at the top of the page. Then have the child draw his or her favorite circus animal and fill in the blanks with a describing word and the animal name. Use page 76 to create a book cover. Collect all the pages and create a class book by binding or stapling the pages together.

2. Show the cover of *See the Circus* and read the title. Ask the children how they think this story will be different from *Paddington Bear at the Circus*. Explain that this is a flap book and the entire picture will not be seen as you are reading.

3. After reading *Paddington Bear at the Circus* and *See the Circus*, compare the likenesses and differences of the stories by completing the Venn Diagram on page 27. Enlarge the Venn diagram onto tag board and laminate it. Use a dry-erase marker to record children's responses. Use a small piece of felt to erase the children's responses on the Venn diagram.

4. Reread *See the Circus*. Ask children to guess what is hiding under the flap before lifting. Follow-up by having the children complete the Riddle Book on page 29. Read each riddle, then have the children illustrate what is being described. Answers are elephant, clown, and lion. To put the book together, cut the pages along the lines, stack them in the correct order and staple.

Overview *(cont.)*

Enjoying the Book *(cont.)*

5. Use the book to teach spatial relationships. Slowly page through the story discussing each character, what he or she is doing and where he or she is (i.e., on the tightrope, beside the ringmaster, next to the bucket, etc.). Give each child a story work mat (page 20, Setting the Stage, #2) and a few animal crackers. Give oral directions as to where to place each cracker (place the lion beside the seal). End the lesson with a yummy treat by allowing the children to eat their animals.

6. Teach the song, "Through the Hoop" (page 62). Sing through several times while children pretend to be tigers. Hold a hula-hoop upright, but still touching the floor. As the song is sung, children crawl around the room in a line, jumping through the hoop as they approach it. You may wish to hang four or five strips of yellow and orange crepe paper from the top of the hula-hoop to simulate a fire ring. Create a hoop and leaping tiger that the children will be able to take home as they share the song (page 59).

7. Check your children's retention of the story by asking the following questions:

- What animal bopped Bobo the boxer in the nose?
- What strong animal held the lady in the air?
- What animal walked on top of the wheel drum?
- In our story, were the bears dancing, sliding, or riding bicycles?
- Who was the lady that walked very carefully and carried an umbrella?
- What animal was good at balancing colored balls on his nose?

   Follow-up by having the children complete page 49.

Extending the Book

1. Review beginning sounds by having the children complete page 38.

2. Enhance your children's small motor, eye/hand coordination skills through a peg board activity. During free exploration time, set out pegboards and copies of page 28 for the children to follow.

3. Ask the children to state the largest animal found in the story (the elephant). Explain that in traveling circuses and in other countries, like India (show on a globe), elephants are used to help do heavy work, like setting up the circus tent, moving logs, etc. Do an Internet search using the words "African elephant," "elephant," "circus elephants," then "pictures," to see these pachyderm pals at work. Create an outdoor circus scene, where the elephant helps to raise the big top. Run one copy per child of page 55 on white construction paper. Each child will need one 9" x 12" (23cm x 30cm) piece of light blue construction paper, one brad, and one 6" (15cm) piece of yarn. Children color and cut out the pieces from page 55. Attach the circus tent to the left side of the blue construction paper using the brad at the marked spot. Tape one end of the piece of yarn to the top of the circus tent and the other end to the elephant's trunk. Children can now use their crayons or colored pencils to draw the background. Walk the elephant across the bottom and up goes the tent!

Overview *(cont.)*

Extending the Book *(cont.)*

4. Generally, children are fascinated with the circus elephants because of their enormous size and since their looks are nothing like that of any other animal of the circus. Introduce the word "pachyderm" to the children. Explain that the first part of the word "pachy" means "thick" and the last part "derm" means "skin"—meaning "thick skinned". Ask the children if they can think of an animal in our story that is a pachyderm (the elephant). Ask if they can think of any other animal that might belong to this group (hippo, rhino). Run one copy of page 42 for each child. Instruct them to look carefully at each animal on the page, deciding which ones are pachyderms, and circle them.

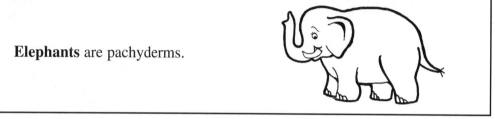

Elephants are pachyderms.

5. Sing the alphabet song with your children, pointing to each letter as it is sung (page 20, Setting the Stage, #1). For a more challenging activity, tell the children that when you sing the song together this time, you will all sing it like a silly clown would by singing it backwards! Again, point to each letter as it is sung. Now, the children can complete the dot-to-dot worksheet on page 37 forward or backward!

6. *See the Circus* is a great book to use to introduce circus occupations to your class. Slowly show the pages of the book to the class, looking at each picture and discussing the characters and their jobs, remembering to talk about the different tools they use and how they dress. After finishing the book, have the children brainstorm for other jobs people might have with the circus (i.e., ticket taker, vendor, feeding the animals, veterinarian, teacher for the children performers, etc.). Write them down on chart paper using a dark marker. Run one copy of page 56 for each child having them match the circus workers with their job.

7. Let's pretend! Follow the instructions on page 67 to make a tightrope for your classroom. Now let the children pretend they are tightrope walkers for the circus. Teach them the poem, "Walking the Tightrope" (page 31), to repeat as they perform. Follow-up by having the children make a picture where the tightrope walker really moves! The directions for this aerial dancer are found on page 61.

8. Enlarge pages 51–53 to create a counting big book, that also rhymes, to share with the children. After enlarging it, color, cut, laminate, and bind the pages together by stapling. Make a corresponding child-size book by duplicating one copy of pages 51–53 for each child. They too, color, cut and bind the pages together by stapling. Variation: Your children will be jumping with excitement when they enter your classroom each day by chanting the rhyme while hopping across a "welcome" mat. Enlarge and color one copy of pages 51-53 on white construction paper. When laminating, feed the pages into the laminator, in line, one in front of the other (much like a sidewalk), beginning with the last (9-10) and ending with the first(1-2). Lay the mat on the floor starting at your doorway and tape it down securely. The children hop, using both feet, on the pages as they say the chant.

22

Overview *(cont.)*

Extending the Book *(cont.)*

9. With the help of the children, make a list of all the animals seen in the story on the board or a large piece of lined paper. Ask the children to think of other animals, that weren't in the story which they might actually see at the circus. List these next to the first list. Explain that many of the animals have babies while they work for the circus. Many times, the babies are trained to work for the circus too. Discuss the animals and the special names for their babies (calf, cub, colt). Run one copy of page 40 for each child to complete as a follow-up activity.

10. There's no place better than the circus for comparing numbers of animals. Enhance your children's graphing skills by duplicating one copy of page 54 for each child. Children simply count the animals in the picture, then, using their crayons, graph accordingly.

11. Teach or review two-color patterning. As a follow-up activity, run one copy of Pachyderm Patterns (page 48) for each child to complete. You may wish to bring the lesson to a close by having the children do the Elephant Walk described on page 67.

12. Enhance your children's vocabulary, spelling, and writing skills by having them complete a story about a trip to the circus. Run one copy of page 36 for each child. Children use the word bank at the bottom of the page to fill in the blanks. Depending on your children's abilities, you may wish to complete this page along and in front of them or place a copy on the overhead and work with them.

13. The circus is not only a sight to behold, but the sounds of the circus are just as exciting. From the beating drums of the circus music, to a seal playing horns, to the roar of the lion, the circus is filled with wonderful sounds! All sound can be traced to the vibration of some material. Some vibrations can be seen, like the vibration of a guitar string when plucked (show children if possible). Some vibrations can be felt, like the vibration of a person's vocal chords (have the children lay their hand on their throat and speak). The same is true for animals, such as, the seal's bark, the monkey's chatter, and the lion's roar (have the children make several animal noises while holding a hand on their throat to feel the vibration). The children can now make a roaring lion of their own demonstrating how "sound is vibration". Each child will need a copy of page 43, on tag board, a paper cup, an 8" (20 cm) piece of string, and a paper clip. Follow the instructions on page 43 to complete this roaring project.

Classroom Activities

Bell-Ringer Activities

Choose one of the following activities to introduce a new concept, review a previous lesson, or simply get the children thinking. These activities are ideal for daily journal writing as well.

1. On the first page of the story, Miss Polly's poodle led the ponies into the circus ring. What would have happened if the poodle had dropped the leash?

2. Turn to the page in the book where the clowns are balancing a chair on a table. Kiki the clown had a pool of water to fall into. Ask the children what would have happened to Kiki if the pool hadn't been there. This is a great lead in to a safety discussion.

3. Have the children name as many of the characters in *See the Circus* as they can remember. You may wish to have them draw a picture of each character and write its name.

4. Have the children describe the different costumes the performers in the circus are wearing.

5. Ask the children why there is a net below the tightrope walkers.

6. There is a character in *See the Circus* that actually comes from another series of books by the author, H. A. Rey. Ask the children if they can figure out who it is (Curious George).

Estimation Ideas

Place a small desk at a convenient spot in the classroom. Supply pencils, sticky notes, a name chart, and one of the ideas listed below (change daily). Children may write their estimations on sticky notes and post them on the name chart as they come in each morning. At some point during the day, find the answer to the problem together. This is a great way to take attendance.

1. Have the children estimate how many crackers are in small box of animal crackers.

2. Fill a small jar with shelled peanuts, popped corn, or candy peanuts. Have the children estimate how many there are.

3. Place pom poms, cotton balls, or balloons in a small clear sandwich bag and have the children estimate how many are inside.

4. Lay a tightrope on the floor or place a hoop on the floor and have the children estimate how many children could fit on the tightrope or inside the circus ring.

Math Story Work Mat

Math Story Work Mat *(cont.)*

Venn Diagram

Teacher Directions: You may wish to enlarge the diagram below onto tag board and laminate. Compare *See the Circus* and *Paddington Bear at the Circus*; record responses on the diagram using a dry-erase marker. A small piece of felt works well to erase the responses when you're finished with the lesson.

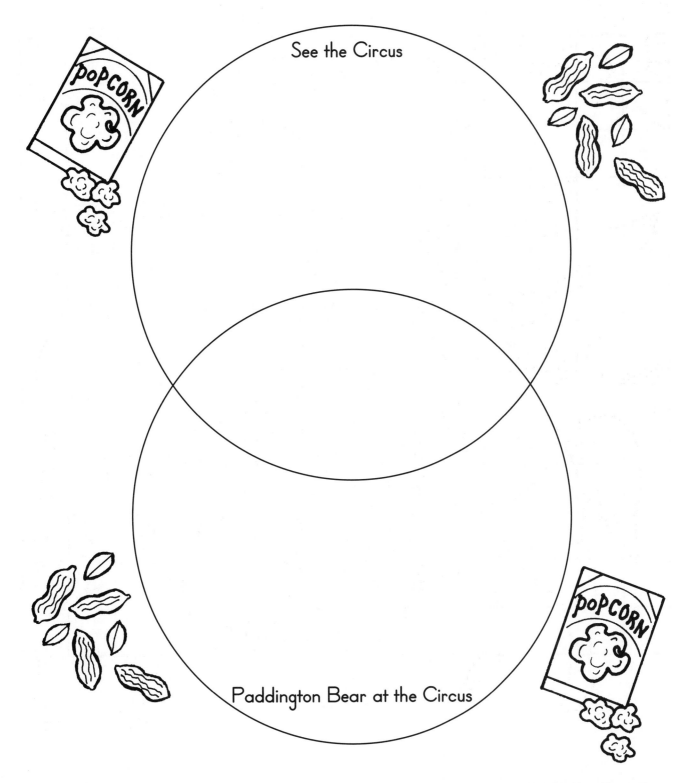

See the Circus

Paddington Bear at the Circus

Pegboard Elephant

Directions: Follow the pattern below to create an elephant on your pegboard.

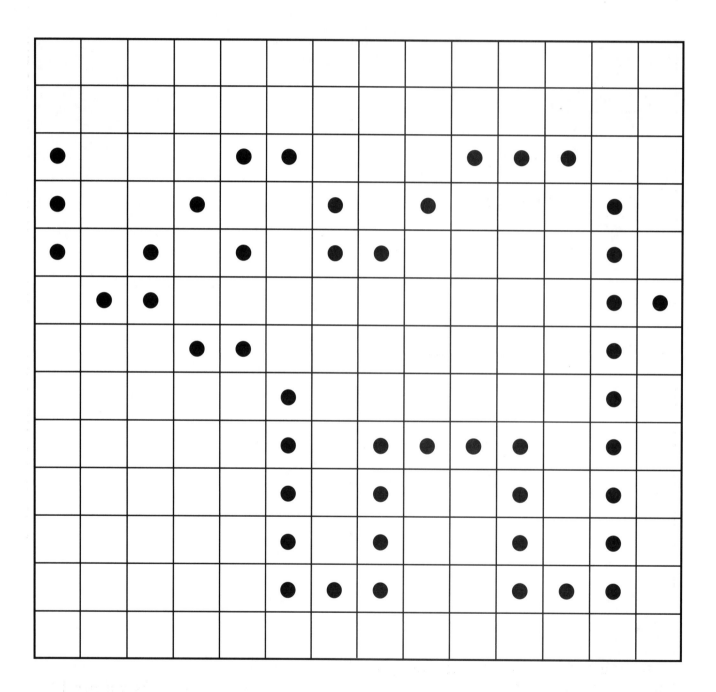

Riddle Book

Directions: Draw the answer to each riddle. Cut apart the pages and staple them together to create a book.

GUESS

WHO?

Name _____

I am very large. I have a trunk. What am I?

2

I have a funny face. I make people laugh. What am I?

3

I roar. I have a mane. What am I?

4

The Circus Wagon Book

What do you see?

I see a

looking at me.

Circus Poems

Clowns

A clown is a person with a silly face,

   Polka-dot pants trimmed in lace.

Big red shoes that flop when they run,

   I think clowns are number one!

Circus Food

Popcorn, ice cream, cotton candy.

   But watch those peanuts, 'cause elephants think they're dandy!

Stilts

(Goes along with *Paddington Bear at the Circus*)

Stilts, stilts, they make you tall.

   Be careful when you walk, so you don't fall.

They're made of wood and make you look

   Like you're standing on a ladder like the clown in this book.

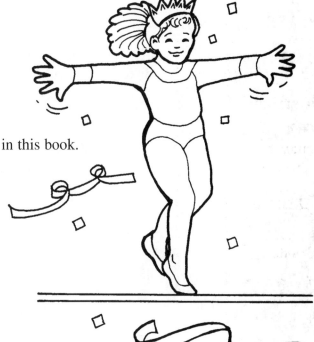

Circus Performers

(Goes along with *See the Circus*)

Terry has his tigers, Polly has her ponies.

   Bobo the boxer got bopped in the nosey!

Miss Lou has her lions, And Fred has his bears.

   The lady on the tightrope is up in the air!

Walking the Tightrope

Walk the tightrope carefully

   It's not that easy, you will see.

Place one foot down on the rope just so

   Put the other foot in front and off you go!

What Makes A Clown

A clown has big feet

   And a nose of red.

And he wears an orange wig

   Upon his head!

Phonemic Activities

What Sound Is Missing?

Give the children a "circus" word and have them repeat it. Then say the word again, this time omitting the initial consonant. Ask the children, "What sound is missing?"

For example, the teacher says, "tiger." Then she says, "iger." Then she asks the students, "What sound is missing?" The students respond, "t."

Syllabication Activity

Have the children clap, tap, or jump out the syllables of the names of many circus workers and animals.

Clown		**train**	**er**		**el**	**e**	**phant**
1		1	+ 1		1	+ 1	+ 1

Where Do You Hear the Sound?

Before beginning this activity, each student will need one index card. Using a marker, make a line down the middle of the card, dividing it in half the short way. Give each child one card and one counter or bingo chip. Instruct the children to listen for a specific sound in a word. The teacher says the word and then asks the children to place their chip where they heard that sound either at the beginning of the word (left side of card), or at the end of the word (right side of card). (For example, the teacher says, "Listen for the **/l/** sound in this word." She then says, "**lion**." The teacher then asks the students to place their chip where they heard the **/l/** sound.")

Silly Sound Substitution!

The teacher says a circus word and the students repeat it, such as "**tiger**." Then, the students are asked to change the **/t/** sound, at the beginning of the word, to a **/p/** sound. The students will love making these nonsense words that rhyme!

Clowning Around with Opposites

Directions:

1. Color all the pictures on the page.
2. Cut apart the pictures at the bottom of the page.
3. Glue the pictures next to the picture that represents its opposite.

wet   tall

big feet   happy

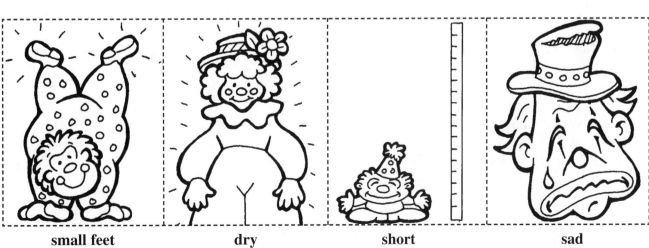

small feet   **dry**   **short**   **sad**

Draw Me a Story

Directions for the Storyteller

As you tell the story "*What I Want To Be*", draw each italic direction onto chart paper using a thick, black marker. Give each child a small chalkboard, dry-erase board, or paper and writing utensil and ask them to be the illustrator during a re-telling of the story. It may help the students to see the teacher drawing on the board along with them.

What I Want To Be

Once upon a time, Sam and Dani, who were the best of friends, heard the circus was in town. (*Draw two stars side by side to represent Sam and Dani.*)

1.

They decided to buy tickets and go see the show. They asked the woman selling tickets where to find the circus. She told them to walk north, to the edge of town and there they would see the large, striped circus tent. (*Draw a pentagon shape with stripes centered above the stars.*)

2.

Once inside the circus tent, Sam and Dani found their seats. They saw a large circus ring in the center of the tent. (*Draw a large circle starting at the bottom of the tent.*)

3.

A man selling cotton candy came around before the show started and Sam and Dani each bought one cone of the candy. (*Draw fluffy cotton candy on each side of the tent.*)

4.

A loud voice, welcoming everyone to the circus, was heard and standing in the middle of the large center ring was the ringmaster. (*Draw a smaller circle in the middle of the large circle, centered underneath the two stars.*)

5.

Sam and Dani saw tigers jumping through hoops, dancing bears, and men on trapeze. But, their favorite part was when a clown slipped on a banana and fell down, knocking all the other clowns down with him. Sam and Dani said, "That's what I want to be when I grow up!" (*Draw a banana shape below the small circle representing the ring master.*)

6.

Ask the students what Sam and Dani wanted to be? **A clown!**

Put On a Happy Face

Directions: Make two blue eyes on the clown. Put polka dots on his pants. Draw orange hair on him. Make a red circle for the clown's nose. Draw three balloons in the clown's hand.

My Trip To the Circus

Directions: Use the word bank at the bottom to fill in the blanks to complete the story.

Today, the _____ came to town. My family went to see the show. I saw an orange and black striped _____ jumping through hoops. Huge _____ walked in a line around the circus ring making noises with their trunks. A pretty lady walked high up in the air on a _____. Then came in a funny _____. The clown threw a _____ at his friend's face. But my favorite was the tall clown walking on _____. I bought a bright red _____ with a string that I could hang on to. I had a great time at the circus!

Word Bank

circus	tiger	tightrope	pie

balloon	elephants	clown	stilts

Dancing Bear

Connect the dots in the order of the alphabet and color the picture.

What Letter Do I Begin With?

Directions: Look at each picture below. Say the word carefully, listening for its beginning sound. Write the letter that each word begins with in the blank provided.

_____ lown

_____ alloons

_____ lephant

_____ eal

_____ ion

_____ ent

_____ ingmaster

_____ ony

Clowning with Ending Sounds

Directions: The objects below represent what a clown would wear. Say the name of each picture carefully, listening for the ending sound. Write the letter that represents the sound that you hear at the end of each word in the space provided.

wi _____

ha _____

dres _____

flowe _____

shir _____

soc _____

make-u _____

pant _____

Help Me Find My Mama

Directions: Circus animals have babies just like farm and forest animals do. Look carefully at the circus animals below and draw a line to match.

Baby Animals   **Adult Animals**

Don't Burst the Balloon!

Balloons are a colorful part of the circus. Often times, they are attached to a child's finger or wrist with a string. In this experiment, the balloon is attached to the top of an empty soda bottle. This teacher directed experiment shows children how a gas which fills the balloon is made by combining some simple kitchen ingredients.

Materials

1 20 oz. (600 ml) empty soda can or water bottle

½ cup (60ml) of vinegar

2 Tbs. (30ml) of baking soda

1 latex balloon

1 small to medium sized funnel

Teacher directions:

Place the funnel in the top of the soda bottle. Pour in the baking soda. Add the vinegar and quickly stretch the balloon over the neck of the bottle. In response to the experiment, ask your students to illustrate what happens to the balloon.

Pachyderm Pals

Directions: Look carefully at each animal. Draw a circle around each animal that is a pachyderm or a "thick-skinned" animal.

The Lion's Roar

Preparation: Tie an 8" (20 cm) piece of string to a paper clip. Poke a small hole in the bottom of a small paper cup and pass the string through the hole. Make one for each child. Demonstrate for your students that "sound is vibration" by creating a roaring lion.

Directions:

1. Color and cut out the lion. Be sure to cut out the mouth of the lion too.

2. Push the cup through the lion's mouth (string in the back).

3. Pull down the length of the string to make the lion roar.

It's Circus Time

Directions: Draw a line from the digital time to the matching face time.

Example:

2:00

6:00

1:00

8:00

3:00

Shape Clown

Directions:

1. Color the shapes below with crayons.

2. Using scissors, cut out the shapes and find the matching one on page 46.

3. Glue each shape where it belongs.

4. Point to and name each shape.

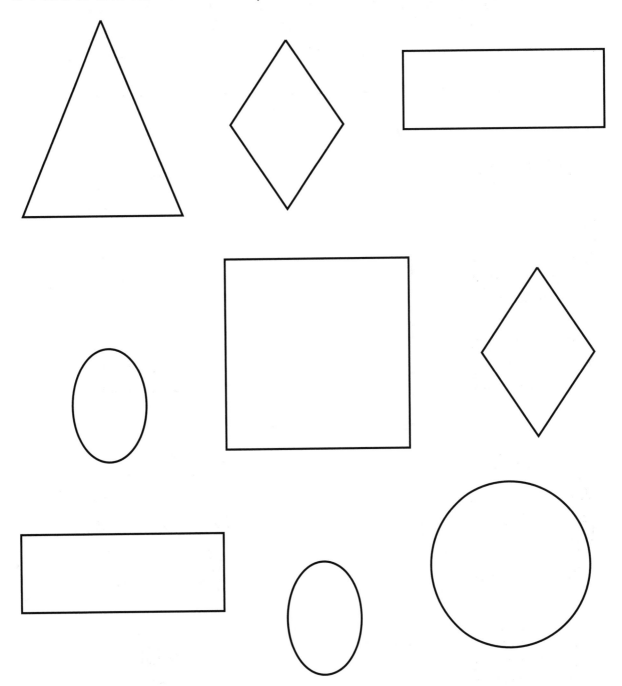

Shape Clown *(cont.)*

46

Clown Costumes

Directions:

1. Using scissors, cut the costume pieces below.

2. Find the piece of clothing with the matching pattern. Glue it in the space provided to complete the costumes. Color the costumes.

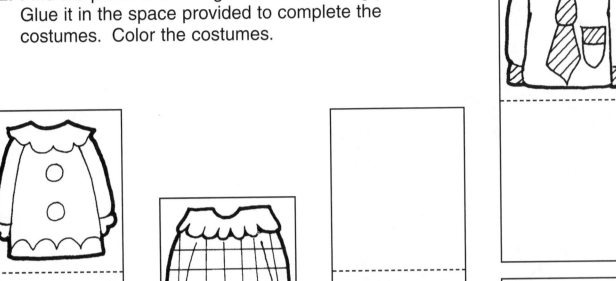

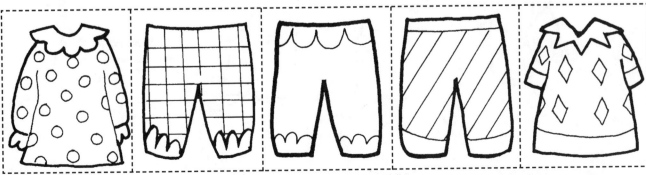

Pachyderm Patterns

Directions: Choose two different colored crayons. Use them to color the elephant's blankets in a pattern.

48

Silly Seal

Directions: Color the picture below using the color code as a guide.

1–red   **2**–blue   **3**–orange   **4**–green   **5**–yellow

Yummy Facts

Directions:

1. Count the circus treats below each number.
2. Add the two groups together.
3. Write the numeral in the box provided.

2   +   3 = ☐   1   +   1 = ☐

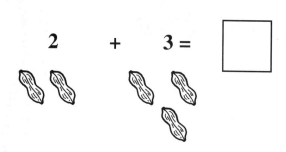   

1   +   4 = ☐   5   +   2 = ☐

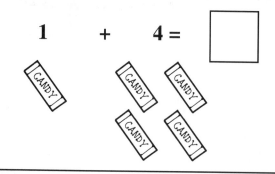   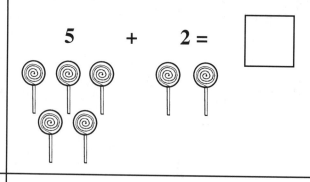

2   +   2 = ☐   3   +   4 = ☐

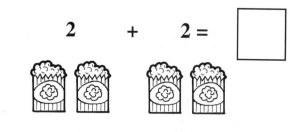   

3   +   3 = ☐   1   +   2 = ☐

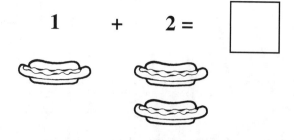

Circus Count Booklet

(Use with pages 52 and 53.)

Counting at the Circus

Name _____

1–2

The clown lost his shoe.

Circus Count Booklet *(cont.)*

(Use with pages 51 and 53.)

3-4

I heard the lion roar!

5-6

Cotton candy on a stick.

Circus Count Booklet *(cont.)*

(Use with pages 51 and 52.)

7–8

The clown spins plates.

9–10

I see a tiger in a pen.

Big Top Graph

Directions: Color one block for each animal seen in the picture above.

A Tent Raising

Materials: (per child)
- one copy of patterns below
- one 9" x 12" (23cm x 30cm) piece of light blue construction paper
- one 6" (15cm) piece of yarn
- one brad
- crayons and scissors

Directions:

1. Color and cut out the circus tent and the elephant.
2. Attach the tent to the left side of the blue construction paper by placing a brad through the "X."
3. Tape one end of the piece of yarn to the top of the tent, the other end to the elephant's trunk.
4. Fill in the background.
5. Walk the elephant across the bottom (to the right) and up goes the tent.

Working at the Circus

Directions: Draw a line matching the circus worker with the job he or she performs.

clown

lion tamer

horse trainer

tightrope walker

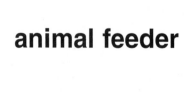

animal feeder

Be a Clown

Being a clown isn't all banana peels and pies in the face. For some people, clowning is their job, therefore, it must be taken seriously. The slips and tumbles and juggling acts all look so easy, but it takes special training and lots of practice to perform these with accuracy. Many jobs require a college education to learn special skills, the same education is required of clowns. Clown colleges, and schools of physical theater and circus arts train clowns to juggle, walk the tightrope, ride unicycles, paint faces, mime, and do acrobatic feats safely. There are even some schools and camps that children may attend.

Directions: Using scissors, cut the picture along the dotted lines to make the circus picture into a puzzle.

Circus Art

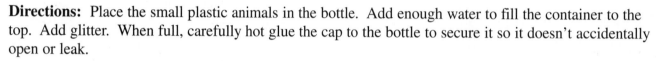

Big Top Bottle

Materials for One Bottle

- one empty 20 oz. (600 ml) soda or water bottle
- small plastic circus animals
- glitter or metallic confetti
- hot glue gun
- water

Directions: Place the small plastic animals in the bottle. Add enough water to fill the container to the top. Add glitter. When full, carefully hot glue the cap to the bottle to secure it so it doesn't accidentally open or leak.

Paper Plate Pachyderm

Materials:

- crayons or markers
- paper plates (two per child)
- 2" x 18" (5cm x 46cm) strips of colored construction paper (one per child)
- scissors
- stapler

Directions: Using crayons or markers, color the paper plate a desired color. Draw eyes and mouth on the front of the plate. Cut the second paper plate in half to make ears. Use a stapler to attach one on each side of the head.

Accordion fold the colored paper strip. Then, using the glue stick, attach it to the center of the plate to represent the elephant's trunk.

High Walkers

Materials:

- two empty coffee cans
- two 6' (182 cm) pieces of twine
- spray paint, your choice of color
- stickers
- one nail and hammer

Directions: Turn the coffee cans upside-down so that they are sitting on their lids. Using the nail and hammer, make two holes, opposite each other, near the tin bottom of the can. Spray paint each can. Use stickers to decorate the can when the paint is dry. Thread one piece of twine through the top of the hole and tie the ends together inside the can. Repeat with the other can. With the cans still inverted, children stand on the can bottoms, hold the string in their hands, and walk.

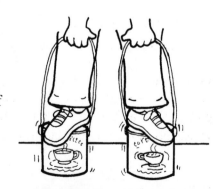

58

Circus Art *(cont.)*

Ringmaster Hatbands

Materials:

- one 3" x 18" (8cm x 46cm) piece of black construction paper strip per child

- one 12" x 18" (30cm x 46cm) piece of black construction paper per child

- white and yellow crayon

- glue stick and stapler

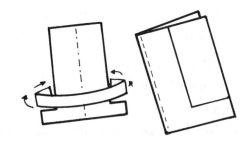

Directions:

Fold the 12" x 18" (30cm x 46cm) piece of construction paper in half. Using a white or yellow crayon, make an "L" shape on the paper staying away from the fold. Cut on the crayon lines. When paper is unfolded, it should look like a top hat. Place the glue along the bottom of the hat shape and attach it to the paper strip. Fit ringmaster hatbands to each child's head and staple.

Leaping Tigers

Materials:

- one copy per child of the tiger pattern (page 73) on white construction paper

- one 9" (23 cm) paper plate

- one 4" (10 cm) length of yarn

- crayons

- scissors

- tape

Directions: Prepare a hoop for the tigers to jump through by cutting out the center of the paper plates to form a ring. Have children color the tiger pattern with crayons and cut it out when finished. Tape one end of the yarn to the inside ring of the plate. Tape the other end to the tiger's back. Now your tiger is leaping through the hoop!

Circus Posters

Materials:

- white construction paper or butcher paper

- water color paints

- markers

- sequins

- glue

Directions: Give each child a piece of paper. Supply various art materials and allow the children to be creative! You may wish to display these as part of the culminating activity. For very young children, print out circus words on the computer and have them decorate or illustrate the poster.

Circus Art *(cont.)*

"Stilts" the Clown

Materials:

- one copy of the legless clown (page 77) and shoes on (page 78) white construction paper
- two 2" x 18" (5 cm x 46 cm) paper strips of various colors
- crayons
- scissors
- glue

Directions: Children color and cut out the clown and shoe shapes. Accordion fold the two paper strips. Place glue on one end of the folded paper strip and attach it to the bottom left side of the clown. Repeat the process with the other paper strip, this time attaching it to the right side. Attach feet to the bottom of the paper strips using glue.

Dough Recipe

Materials:

- 1 cup (225g) flour
- 1 cup (225g) salt
- ½ cup (120mL) water
- medium-sized bowl
- wooden spoon
- zipper plastic bag

Directions: Mix the flour, salt, and water together in a medium-sized bowl using a wooden spoon. After initial mixing, finish the dough by kneading it with your hands on a lightly floured surface until not sticky. Keep prepared dough in a zipper plastic bag until ready to use. Use the dough to create circus animals.

Circus Art (cont.)

Movable Tightrope Walker Picture
(sliding strip page)

Materials:

- 8 ½" x 11" (22cm x 28cm) light construction paper, one per child
- tightrope walker pattern (page 75), one per child
- markers, colored pencils, or crayons
- tag board
- utility knife and scissors (adult use only)
- glue

Directions:

1. Give each student a piece of construction paper.

2. Draw a line, 7" (18cm) in length across the top of the paper, approximately 3" (8cm) from the top edge.

3. Cut the line with a utility knife, beginning one inch (3cm) in from the edge and ending one inch from the other edge. This is your large slot. See diagram.

4. Cut a small vertical slot 1 ⅛" (3cm) long near the end of the large slot (right side).

5. Color and cut out the tightrope walker pattern (page 75).

6. Create a sliding strip to help the tightrope walker gracefully dance across the page by cutting a piece of tagboard 5 ½" x ¾" (14cm x 2cm). Cut a tab 1 ½" x ¼" (4cm x.6cm), using tagboard. Glue the bottom half of the tab to the left side of your strip. Fold the rest of the tab down on itself.

7. Slip the strip through the small slot. Pull the loose part of the tab through the large slot. Fold the end of the tab upward on the tab's fold line. Make sure the fold line of your tab is on the large slot.

8. Apply glue to the top of your folded tab. Place your tightrope walker on the glued tab, make sure you do not glue your figure to the page. Allow glue to dry before pulling the strip.

9. Cut the end of the strip to make it shorter, if necessary. Your tightrope walker should now move easily across the large slot of your paper. Have the children draw poles to hold the tightrope, a net, and other circus characters at the bottom of the page.

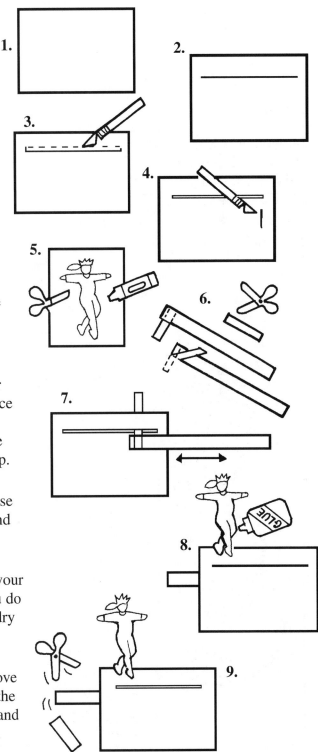

Circus Songs

Under the Big Top

(Sung to the tune of "Up On The House Top")

Under the big top the ring master calls,
    Boys and girls, come one, come all.
See lions, and elephants, and chimpanzees
    Bears and clowns and the man on
    the trapeze.
Dancing dogs, colored balloons,
    Unicycles and baboons.
Under the big top, Oh such fun!
    Now the circus is all done!

The Circus Is In Town

(Sung to the tune of "Mary Had A Little Lamb")

When the circus comes to town, comes to
    town, comes to town.
When the circus comes to town, be sure to go
    see it!
You'll see lots of silly clowns, silly clowns,
    silly clowns.
You'll see lots of silly clowns, be sure to go and
    see it!

Go To The Circus

*(Sung to the tune of
"Row, Row, Row Your Boat")*

Go! Go! To the circus
    When it comes to town.
See lions, bears, and tigers too
    The best show all around.

It's Here Again!

(Sung to the tune of "Pop Goes the Weasel")

The circus comes but once a year
    By wagons, trucks, and trains.
With trainers, clowns, and acrobats
    Yea! It's here again!
The lions, bears, and elephants
    Zebras and monkeys too.
They are coming to your town
    Yea! To see you!

Through the Hoop

(Sung to the tune of "Looby Lou")

The tigers jump through the hoop,
    The tigers jump through the hoop,
The tigers jump through the hoop,
    All on a circus night.
They put their front feet through,
    They jump their back feet through,
They run and leap and make a loop,
    Then jump back through the hoop.

H-A-P-P-Y

(Sung to the tune of "Bingo")

I know a funny little clown
    And Happy is his name-o!
H-A-P-P-Y, H-A-P-P-Y, H-A-P-P-Y
    And Happy is his name-o!

Big Top Recipes

Yummy Animals

- two vanilla wafer cookies per child
- animal crackers
- canned frosting
- food coloring

Directions:

1. Add a few drops of food coloring to the frosting.
2. Spread a small amount on one wafer, lay other wafer on top like a sandwich.
3. Place a dab of frosting on top of the sandwich cookie. Stand an animal cracker in it.

Clowny Cones

- paper bowls or plates
- ice cream scoop
- vanilla ice cream
- sugar cones
- flavored syrup
- candy coated chocolates

Directions:

1. Place one scoop of ice cream in bowl or on plate.
2. Drizzle a small amount of flavored syrup on top, allowing it to run down one side of ice cream. The syrup should not run down over front where the face is.
3. Place sugar cone on top of, and slightly off to one side of ice cream for the clown's hat.
4. Now use candies to make the face!

Ha! Ha! Toast

- milk
- food coloring
- white bread
- new paintbrushes
- butter
- knife
- toaster

Directions:

1. Mix two drops of food coloring with one teaspoon of milk, make several colors.
2. Allow children to paint pictures on a piece of white bread, being careful not to make bread soggy.
3. Toast on normal setting.
4. Butter the toast and enjoy.

Carnival Corn

- popcorn popper
- popping corn
- spray butter or melted butter
- food coloring

Directions:

1. Use popcorn popper to pop corn.
2. Pour into a bowl and let cool.
3. Add food coloring to butter. Mix well and pour over popped corn. Salt if desired.

Big Top Recipes *(cont.)*

Clown Sandwiches

- one slice of bread
- round cookie cutter
- peanut butter
- clean craft sticks
- shredded carrots
- one apple wedge
- one cherry
- two raisins

Directions:

1. Cut a circle shape from the bread with cookie cutter.
2. Spread the peanut butter on the bread with a craft stick.
3. Sprinkle the top of the circle with the carrots to look like hair, use the raisins for eyes, the cherry for a nose, and the apple wedge for a mouth.
* Check for peanut allergies.

Circus Wagon Treats

- one rectangle of graham cracker
- clean craft sticks
- vanilla frosting
- two round sandwich cookies
- animal crackers
- four black licorice pieces cut into 2" (6 cm) pieces

Directions:

1. Using the craft sticks, spread frosting on cracker.
2. Place the round sandwich cookies on the bottom of the cracker to look like wheels.
3. Place an animal cookie in the wagon.
4. Give each student four licorice pieces to place over the top to create the look of a cage.

Tiger Tarts

- refrigerated sugar cookie dough, in ⅓" slices. (1cm)
- vanilla frosting
- raisins
- six 2" (5cm) pieces of black shoe string licorice
- ½ cherry
- clean craft sticks
- oven and cookie sheet

Directions:

1. Each child will need one slice of cookie dough for the tiger head. Divide remaining slices of dough into quarters. Each child needs two quarters to attach to the top of the circle piece for ears.
2. Place the cookies on the cookie sheet and bake according to the package directions. Allow the cookies to cool.
3. Mix food coloring into frosting to create an orange color. Frost the cookies using the craft sticks.
4. Decorate the cookies using two raisins for eyes, one raisin for the nose, one cherry piece for the mouth, and six small pieces of licorice for whiskers.

Circus Games

Clowning Around Relay

Materials:

- small adult or large youth sized clothing —shirt, pants, tie, shoes or slippers, and hat (two of each)

- two clothes baskets or crates

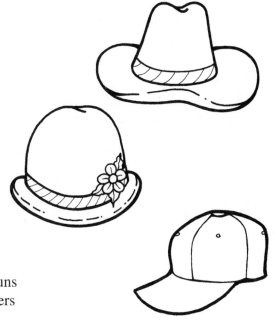

Directions:

Place one set of clothing in each basket or crate. Divide class into two teams. Half of each team lines up on one side of the classroom, while the rest of the team lines up across from them on the other side of the room. Place one basket of clothes in front of the start of each team. The first child in line quickly dresses in the clothing and runs across the room to his or her teammates. He or she then takes the clothing off and the teammate puts them on and runs back to the other side. This continues until all members of the team have had a turn.

Heads Up, Clowns Up
(Similar to Heads-up, 7-Up)

Materials:

- five copies of the clown pattern on page 74

- crayons and scissors

Directions:

Color, cut out, and laminate five clown patterns from page 74. Call five children to the front of the classroom and hand each a clown. Instruct the remaining children in their seats to put their heads down and the close their eyes. While heads are down, each of the five children holding a clown tip-toe around the room and lays his or her clown down beside one child, then returns to front of the room. The teacher then calls, "Heads up, clowns up!" At this time, the five children who were given a clown, stand up. The five chosen children try to guess who gave them the clown. If he or she guesses correctly, they get to switch places with that child. If his or her guess is incorrect, he or she has to sit back down and the game continues.

Circus Games *(cont.)*

Circus Charades

Materials:

- one copy of the animal and performer patterns (page 73-75), reduced in size
- balloons

Directions:

1. Cut out the pattern shapes, fold them up, and place them inside the balloons.

2. Blow up the balloons and tie them shut.

3. Call on one child to break a balloon. The child looks at the picture and, without a sound, acts out what the picture does. The rest of the class guesses at what he or she is pretending to be. The child who guesses correctly gets to pop his or her balloon next.

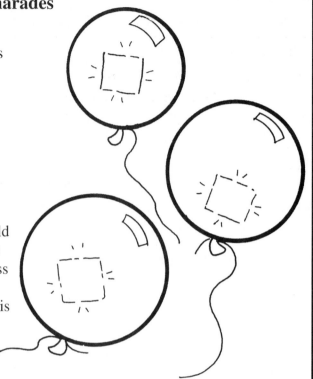

The Great Peanut Race

Materials:

- one drinking straw per child
- peanuts in shell

Directions:

1. Using chalk or masking tape, make a "starting" and "finishing" line on a tabletop or floor.

2. Divide the class into four teams. The first person in line places his or her peanut on the "starting" line.

3. He or she blows air through their straw and moves the peanut toward the "finish" line.

4. The first child to get his or her peanut across the "finish" line wins!

Variation: Make an elephant's trunk shape from gray construction paper (two needed). Laminate and adhere to the top of a ruler. Two children play the game at one time. Each child holds the "elephant's trunk" in one hand. Lay a peanut on the end. Children race to the "finish" line while balancing the peanut on the trunk

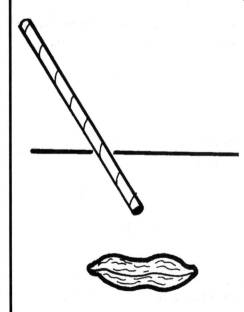

Rhymes, Games, and Activities

Jump Rope Rhymes

Use these rhymes when you jump rope.

Colored Balls

Seals balance balls upon their nose
    Green ones, blue ones, and there's rose.
Toss them up high and catch them down low
    How many balls can they catch in a row?
(1,2,3, count the jumps.)

Pachyderms

Pachyderms, pachyderms all in a row
    Trunks holding tails, swinging to and fro.
They march in a line around the ring
    How many elephants did the circus bring?
(1,2,3 count the jumps.)

Games

Bucket Balance Relay
Materials:

- one plastic sand bucket
- one empty paper towel tube with a hole punched at one end
- one 2' (61cm) length of yarn
- stickers or markers

Teacher Preparation:

Tie one end of the yarn to the bucket handle, and the other through the hole in the paper towel tube. Decorate the paper towel tube with stickers or markers.

Directions: Divide the class in half. Half of the children line up at one end of the classroom, the other half line up directly across from them. Set the bucket on top of the paper towel tube. Hand the tube and bucket to the first child. Children quickly walk across the room while balancing the bucket and pass it off to the next child in line. The game is complete when all the children have participated.

Circus Sound Tag

Directions: This game is played like "freeze" tag. Choose one child to be the ringmaster or "it." All other children run around the gym, or the playground, trying to avoid being touched by the ringmaster. The ringmaster names an animal when he or she touches a child. The child caught, freezes in place and he or she must make that animals' sound twice, before moving. Choose a new ringmaster every few minutes.

Activities

Elephant Walk

Directions: Line up children. Have them bend over, swinging one arm in front like a trunk, the other swinging behind like a tail. Have them grab each other's tails with their trunks and walk slowly around the room.

Tightrope Walking

Directions: Purchase a 15' (5m) long rope. Lay the rope on the floor and allow the children to pretend that they are the aerial dancers of the circus. Variation: Use a balance beam instead, to simulate the tightrope.

Juggling

Directions: Place a crate or basket in the classroom with objects the children can use to juggle with. Some ideas: ping pong balls, scarves, bean bags, empty 20 oz. (600ml) water bottle filled with metallic confetti.

Directions for Culminating Activity

The Circus is in Town

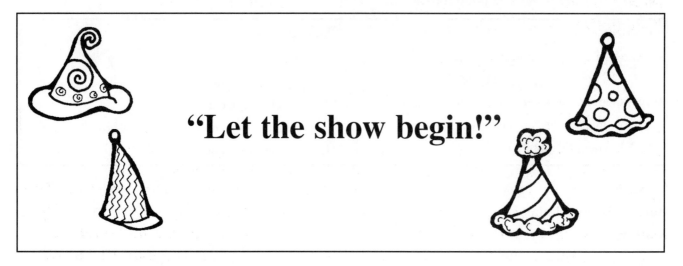

"Let the show begin!"

Teacher Preparation:

1. Prior to this activity, display your student's art work in the hallway and classroom, such as; the "tall" clown (page 6), Enjoying the Book, (#5), and circus posters, (page 59). You may want to decorate with brightly colored balloons too.

2. Have a rope or balance beam ready to use for the tightrope walkers and a hula-hoop for the tigers. Also have bean bags, scarves, or empty soda bottles handy for the juggling act.

3. Use clothes from the Clowning Around Relay (page 65) or washable markers to dress up your class clowns. Washable face paint may be used to make stripes on faces to resemble tigers. Empty aluminum pie tins and bouquets of silk flowers may be used as props for the clowns.

4. Fill out, copy, and send out invitations, (page 79) to parents or other classrooms.

5. You may decide to serve refreshments following the performance. Choose from a variety of recipes on pages 63 and 64. Send copies of the recipe home with students so they can make them again with their families.

6. Look carefully through the play (pages 69 and 70) and choose parts for the children. Groups of children will do that which is bulleted.

7. You may wish to ask a few older students to help with costumes and prop moving during the performance.

8. Have the children learn and practice the songs and poems used in the play in advance.

9. Use chalk or tape to make a large circle on the floor as a focal point or center ring.

10. Ask for help finding circus music from your school music teacher, or see the bibliography on page 80. The music may be played as visitors enter the room and during performances.

The Circus is in Town

Narrator: Come one, come all! Our great circus show is about to begin! Please make way as our performers enter the circus ring in the "Circus Parade of Stars."

- Play circus music as the children parade through the classroom.
- The children stop at the circus ring area and sing, "The Circus is in Town"
- Children exit.

Narrator: The circus has been entertaining crowds for many years. The first circus was held in Pompey's Rome with lions, horses, elephants, and chariot racing. But, as the dark ages settled into Europe, the circus was forgotten. The excitement of the circus was rekindled by a man named Sergeant-Major Philip Astley. He was a talented officer in the British Cavalry who was taken by the excitement of performing fancy riding. Interchanging the equestrian tricks with clown acts, Astley became the creator of our modern circuses.

After the War of 1812, the old style, permanent shows were replaced by traveling circuses. Whether by wagon, truck, or train, the circus was on the move and growing bigger and better along the way. Circus owners purchased exotic animals from the wilds of many countries. And speaking of "wild animals," beware! Here come the terrifying tigers of room _____.

- Fire hoops (hula hoops decorated with paper fire) set up.
- Tigers enter and perform while *Through the Hoop* is sung.
- Tigers exit to circus music.

Narrator: One of the most well known names associated with the circus is P. T. Barnum. Early on, Barnum stimulated the curiosity of his audiences with humans having unusual qualities. From a woman claiming to be 161 years old and the nurse of George Washington, to his good friend Tom Thumb. One of his biggest came in 1882, when be obtained Jumbo the elephant. Elephants have been a long time favorite of circus goers. The enormous pachyderm is a talented performer, and a big help when it comes to doing heavy work. Elephants have been used to move logs, and even help in setting up the circus tent. Please make way for our prized pachyderms!

The Circus is in Town *cont.)*

- Elephants enter doing the "elephant walk" to circus music.

- You may wish to have a ringmaster stand in front of the animals to direct them. When he raises his hands up, the elephants sit and raise their trunks, when he moves his hands in a stirring motion, the elephants turn around.

- Children stop performing and recite the jump rope rhyme, *Pachyderm*. Have them stop jumping at 10.

- Elephants exit to circus music.

Narrator: You've seen a few of the animals showcased in the circus, but we can't forget the talented people involved in the show. These individuals have trained at schools for circus arts and physical theater and they go through rigorous practice sessions. One of the most exciting acts of the circus belongs to the people who walk the tightrope. Please put your hands together as our own very balanced performers dance their way across the high wire.

- Set up balance beams and/or ropes.

- Tightrope walkers enter reciting "Walk the Tightrope."

- Tightrope walkers perform, and then exit.

Narrator: The circus has given us years of enjoyment and many moments to remember. Especially when it comes to clowns. Clowns make us giggle, laugh, and simply, make us happy. Clowns attend schools for circus arts or Clown College. They learn juggling skills, mime, how to ride a unicycle, make-up art, and how to do all their slips and tumbles safely. Send in the clowns!

- Clowns enter and perform a variety of acts (juggling, pie throwing, tumbling)

- Children sing, "H-A-P-P-Y"

Narrator: When the circus comes to your hometown, be sure to go see it. You'll be glad you did.

- Children sing, "Under the Big Top"

Circus Bulletin Boards

Under the Big Top

This bulletin board is a great way to introduce your circus unit. It also goes great with the story *See the Circus* because it is a "lift-the-flap" bulletin board just like the book. Cover the bulletin board twice, using two different colors of butcher paper. Now enlarge the circus tent pattern (page 55) and animal patterns (pages 73-75). Color, cut out, and laminate the pieces. Staple the circus tent to the board. In the opening of the tent, cut a small door shape (three sided) in the first layer of butcher paper using a utility knife. Hold flap back as you staple an animal or performer to the bottom layer of the board. Close the flap. Continue this process until tent in filled. Sing "Under the Big Top" as you show your class this interactive bulletin board.

The Circus Is In Town

Show your class the way the circus moved from town to town, many years ago, by creating this three-dimensional circus wagon train. You will need your children's help. Run several copies of the animal patterns on pages 73-75. Allow children to choose an animal to color and cut out. Give each child one rectangular shaped meat tray. Children glue their animal shape inside the meat tray. You will need to cut four or five slits, directly across from each other, along the top and bottom of the meat trays. Tape a 36" (91cm) length of yarn to the back of the tray at one end. Children wind the yarn around the tray, using the slits as guides, to simulate the bars on a cage. Add paper wheels. Now staple, or pin, wagons to your bulletin board in a line.

Activity Centers

- Set out a variety of materials for a counting and sorting activity. Provide one or more of the following objects: peanuts in the shell, assorted colored balloons, or small animals you would find in a circus. An egg carton works well for sorting.

- Create a circus dollhouse for the children to play with. Use a round, plastic, clothes basket as the circus tent base. Turn the basket upside-down, and using scissors, cut almost half of the basket frame away forming a doorway. Using a large, striped bath towel, create the circus tent. Fold the towel in half and hand or machine stitch one seam together. Turn it so the seam is inside, and wrap it around the basket. To make the tent the correct length, lift towel from the top to the desired length and rubber band it shut. You may wish to hide the rubber band by tying a colorful ribbon or scarf around it. Create a trapeze using a 4" (10cm) long dowel with yarn tied to the ends. Tape yarn strands to the basket bottom that is now the tent top. Purchase plastic animals and people to use in your Circus Tent. If unable to purchase characters, run copies of the animal and people patterns, on pages 73-75, on white construction paper. Color, cut out, and laminate them.

- Help your children review beginning sounds. Run one copy of each animal pattern from pages 73-75. Color, cut out, and laminate it. Write the letter that each animal begins with on separate index cards. Children match the index cards with the correct animals. Store the center in a large envelope.

- To review numbers zero to five. Run six copies of the elephant pattern on page 55. Using a black marker, write one number on each elephant, using the numbers zero to five. Color, cut out, and laminate the elephants. Children could use peanuts in the shell as counters.

- A "Circus" reading area can be made by draping one or two striped sheets over desks or bookcases creating a tent effect. Place circus theme books inside, along with three or four funny clown hats. Use the hats to help monitor the number of children in the center.

- Set out pegboards and copies of the elephant pattern on page 28. Children use the pattern to make the elephant, or simply allow them to try to make different circus animals or clown faces on the pegboards.

- Children enjoy retelling stories. Create a flannel board story telling center by running one copy of pages 73-75. Color, cut out, laminate the characters. Then back the characters with pieces of flannel and store in a see-through plastic bag.

- This center will make the children giggle. Cut a circle with a diameter of 12" (30cm), from cardboard faced with flannel or felt. Cut several eye, nose, and mouth shapes from magazine pictures and laminate them. Back each picture with felt. Tie pieces of yarn together to look like hair. Store the small pieces in a see-through bag and the large circle shape in a pizza box. This would also be a great tool to use when teaching a unit on feelings.

Circus Patterns

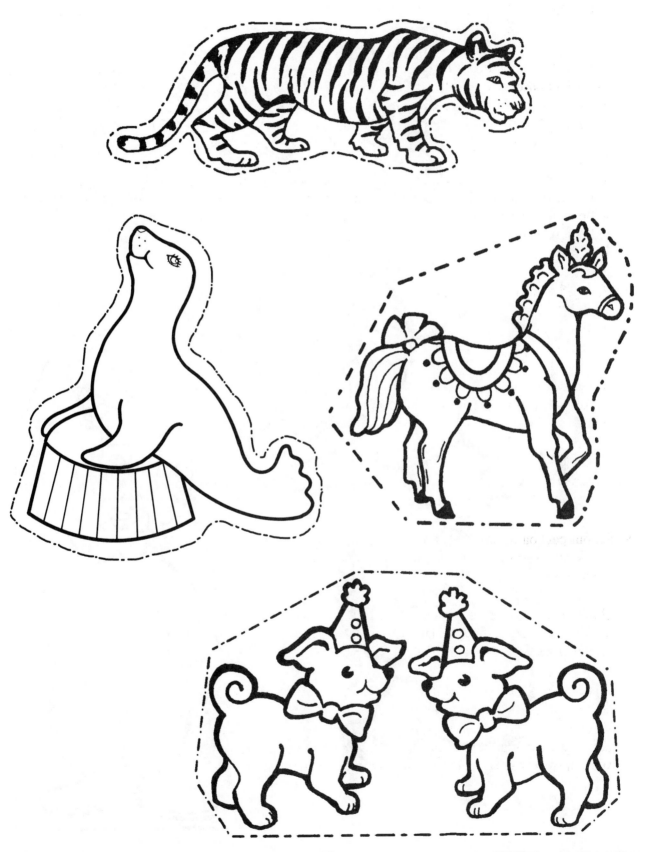

Circus Patterns *(cont.)*

Circus Patterns (cont.)

Circus Patterns *(cont.)*

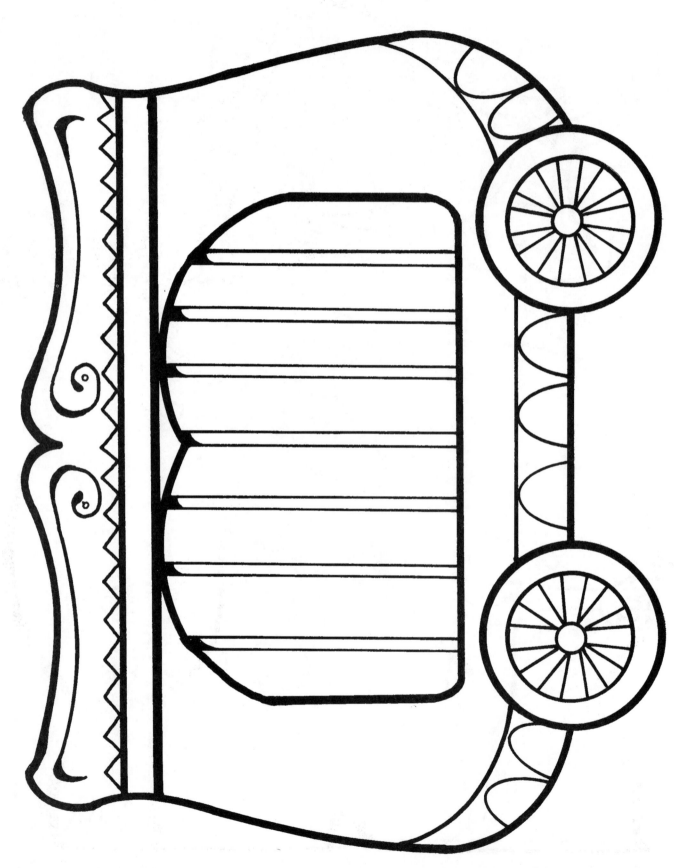

Circus Patterns *(cont.)*

Circus Patterns *(cont.)*

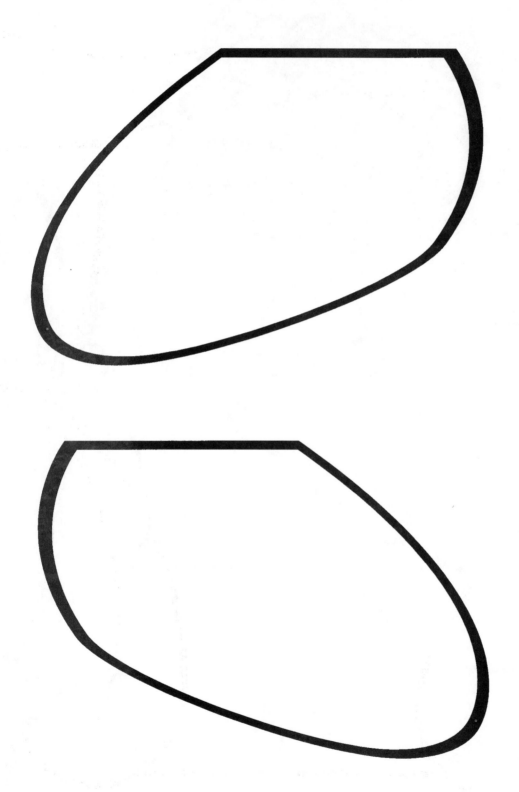

Circus Play

Invitation

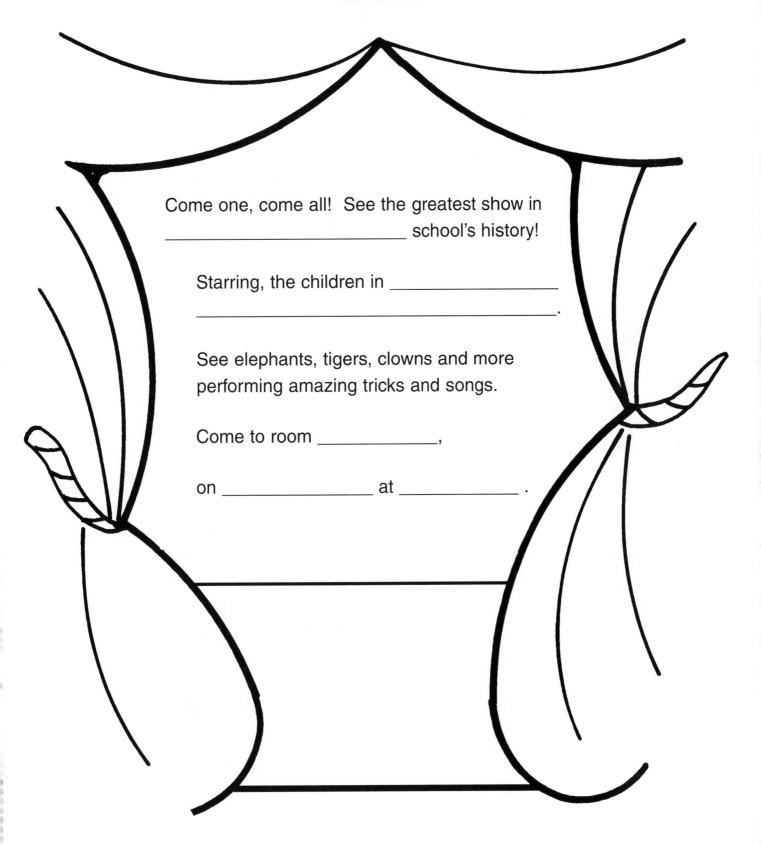

Come one, come all! See the greatest show in
_____ school's history!

Starring, the children in _____

_____.

See elephants, tigers, clowns and more
performing amazing tricks and songs.

Come to room _____,

on _____ at _____ .

Bibliography

Books

Berenstain, Jan and Stan. *The Berenstain's C Book.* Random House, Incorporated, 1997.

Bond, Michael. *Paddington Bear at the Circus.* HarperCollins Children's Books, 2000.

Bridwell, Norman. *Clifford at the Circus.* Scholastic, Incorporated, 1988.

Chwast, Seymour. *The Twelve Circus Rings.* Harcourt, 1996.

Davenport, Meg. *Circus!* Simon and Schuster Children's, 1998.

Doolittle, June. *Circus Train.* Simon and Schuster Children's, 1999.

Ehlert, Lois. *Circus.* HarperCollins Children's Books, 1992.

Freeman, Don. *Bearymore.* Penguin Putnam Books of Young Readers, 1978.

Halsey, Megan. *Circus 1-2-3.* HarperCollins Children's Books, 2000.

Hillert, Margaret. *It's Circus Time, Dear Dragon.* Modern Curriculum, 1984.

Johnson, Crockett. *Harold's Circus.* HarperCollins Children's Books, 1981.

Langen, Annette. *Felix Joins the Circus.* Abbeville Press, Inc., 2000.

Lemelman, Martin. *Circus Opposites.* Innovative Kids, 2000.

Lopshire, Robert. *New Tricks I Can Do.* Random House, Incorporated, 1996.

Paxton, Tom. *Engelbert Joins the Circus.* Morrow, William, and Company, 1997.

Priceman, Marjorie. *Emeline at the Circus.* Random House, Incorporated, 1999.

Rey, H.A. *See the Circus.* Houghton Mifflin Company, 1998.

Spier, Peter. *Peter Spier's Circus!* Bantam Doubleday Dell Publishing Group, 1995.

Suess, Dr. *If I Ran the Circus.* Random House, Incorporated, 1976.

Tibo, Gilles. *Simon at the Circus.* Tundra Books of Northern New York, 1997.

Vincent, Gabrielle. *Ernest and Celestine at the Circus.* Greenwillow Books, 1989.

Wiscman, Bernard. *Morris and Borris at the Circus.* Harper Collins, 1990.

Circus Music

Brass Whistles On Parade. Tangley Calliope. Audio CD. December 1997.

Circus Clown Calliope. Vol. 1 and 2. Audio CD. November 1999.

Circus Music from the Big Top. Merle Evans Circus Band. Audio CD. September 1992.

Circus Spectacular. Matthew H. Phillips and His Circus Band. Audio CD. March 1997.

The Grand Old Circus Band. Audio CD. November 1997.

Circus Links

Allen and Brenda's Circus Photo Journal
    http://www.ov2000.com/circus/

Barnum, P. T.—RBBB Tribute
    http://www.ringling.com

A Brief History of the Circus
    http://www.bigapplecircus.org

Circus Icons
    http://www.cstone.net/~bry-back/iconfun/ circusicons.html

Circus Lingo
    http://www.bigtop.com/kid/lingo.html

The Great Circus Parade-History
    http://www.circusparade.com